My First Animal Library

Bald Eagles

by Mari Schuh

Bullfrog
Books

Ideas for Parents and Teachers

Bullfrog Books let children practice reading informational text at the earliest reading levels. Repetition, familiar words, and photo labels support early readers.

Before Reading

- Discuss the cover photo. What does it tell them?
- Look at the picture glossary together. Read and discuss the words.

Read the Book

- "Walk" through the book and look at the photos. Let the child ask questions. Point out the photo labels.
- Read the book to the child, or have him or her read independently.

After Reading

- Prompt the child to think more. Ask: Have you ever seen a bald eagle? What was it doing?

Bullfrog Books are published by Jump!

5357 Penn Avenue South
Minneapolis, MN 55419
www.jumplibrary.com

Copyright © 2016 Jump! International copyright reserved in all countries. No part of this book may be reproduced in any form without written permission from the publisher.

Library of Congress Cataloging-in-Publication Data

Schuh, Mari C., 1975– author.
  Bald eagles / by Mari Schuh.
      pages cm. — (My first animal library)
  Audience: Ages 5–8.
  Audience: K to grade 3.
  Includes index.
  ISBN 978-1-62031-287-2 (hardcover: alk. paper) —
  ISBN 978-1-62496-347-6 (ebook)
  1. Bald eagle—Juvenile literature. I. Title.
  II. Series: Bullfrog books. My first animal library.
  QL696.F32S33 2016
  598.9'42—dc23
                                          2015026140

Editor: Jenny Fretland VanVoorst
Series Designer: Ellen Huber
Book Designer: Michelle Sonnek
Photo Researcher: Michelle Sonnek

Photo Credits: All photos by Shutterstock except:
Dreamstime, 19, 23tl; Getty, 20–21; iStock, 1;
Thinkstock, 8–9, 12, 23br.

Printed in the United States of America at
Corporate Graphics in North Mankato, Minnesota.

Table of Contents

High in the Sky

A bald eagle soars.

It flies high in the sky.

Long wings help it soar.
Brown feathers cover
its body and wings.

Look at its head.

It is not bald.

It has white feathers.

9

The bald eagle sits
on a perch.

It looks for prey.

It can see a long way.

perch

Wow! A fish!
The eagle dives.
It is fast.

Its talons grab the fish.

Got it!

The eagle flies to a tree.

Time to eat!

It uses its beak.

Yum!

beak

The eagle builds a nest.

It adds sticks.

It is big.

See the eggs?

They hatch.
Look at the eaglets!

eaglets

19

The eaglets grow.

They will fly high in the sky, too.

Parts of a Bald Eagle

eyes
Bald eagles have excellent eyesight; they can see better than people can.

feathers
Brown feathers cover a bald eagle's body and wings.

beak
A strong, hooked beak helps a bald eagle rip its food.

talons
Sharp talons grab and hold onto prey.

tail
Bald eagles have white feathers on their tails.

Picture Glossary

eaglets
Young bald eagles; eaglets are also called chicks.

prey
Animals that are hunted for food.

perch
A high place where a bird can sit.

soar
To fly or glide high in the air.

Index

To Learn More

Learning more is as easy as 1, 2, 3.

1) Go to www.factsurfer.com

2) Enter "baldeagles" into the search box.

3) Click the "Surf" button to see a list of websites.

With factsurfer.com, finding more information is just a click away.